LD:

98
678s

Cohen, Daniel.
    Supermonsters / Daniel Cohen. -- New
York : Dodd, Mead, c1977.
    128 p. : ill, ; 22 cm.
    Includes index.
    SUMMARY: Discusses the history of a
variety of monsters including vampires,
werewolves, and zombies.

    1. Monsters.   I. Title

21 SEP 82   2542972 CRP5xc   76-48970

SUPERMONSTERS

SUPERMONSTERS

**Daniel
Cohen**

Illustrated with photographs and prints

DODD, MEAD & COMPANY

New York

The following illustrations are used by permission and through the courtesy of: Culver Pictures, Inc., 18, 56, 84; The Metropolitan Museum of Art, photograph by Harry Burton, 65; Whitney Gallery of Western Art, Cody, Wyoming, 67.

3   4   5   6   7   8   9   10

Library of Congress Cataloging in Publication Data

Cohen, Daniel.
  Supermonsters.

  Includes index.
  SUMMARY: Discusses the history of a variety
of monsters including vampires, werewolves, and
zombies.
    1. Monsters — Juvenile literature. [1. Monsters]
I. Title.
GR825.C493   398'.45   76-48970
ISBN 0-396-07399-9

To Howard Smith

CONTENTS

SUPERMONSTERS

Dracula, the vampire

1

THE MONSTERS AWAKE

The coffin lid swings slowly open. A figure rises from its dark interior. His face is strangely pale. His teeth are unusually long. They glitter in a shaft of moonlight that streams into the crypt. The figure steps out of the coffin. He spreads his dark cloak at arm's length. Suddenly he is gone. A large bat hovers where the figure once stood. Who is it? Why Dracula, of course.

The forest is shrouded in mist. But through the mist one can see the moon is full. In the distance there is an animal-like howling. Something moves. It comes closer quietly and quickly. The creature moves with the grace of an animal, yet it walks on two legs. Finally it creeps close enough to see its horrible, hairy face. It is the Wolf Man.

Lightning flashes around the castle. In an enormous vaulted chamber two men are at work. They are twisting dials and throwing switches on complicated machinery. The power of the lightning is carried down wires into the machinery. From the machinery more wires lead to a table covered by a sheet. Something stirs under the sheet. The sheet falls away, revealing a monster. Slowly the monster rises from the table. With a terrible effort it breaks the shackles that hold it.

The waters of the harbor seem calm and peaceful. Suddenly there is a great disturbance. From out of the foam steps a huge green dinosaur. It is at least 500 feet tall. People scream and rush away. They know that Godzilla is about to attack their city.

Dracula, the Wolf Man, the Frankenstein monster, Godzilla—they are some of the monsters

12

The Wolf Man, from the movie *Curse of the Werewolf*

Godzilla

you will meet in the pages of this book. You are also likely to meet them in your movie theatre, on your television set, and in other books. They are the Supermonsters.

At one time people believed in some of these monsters. A lot of people were genuinely afraid of vampires. People were executed because other people thought they were werewolves. Vampires and werewolves didn't exist, but people thought they did.

Some of the other monsters were never really believed in. Godzilla was created in a movie studio in Japan in 1955. No one ever pretended that such a monster really existed.

But whether they believed in them or not, people have always been fascinated by monsters. I don't know why we enjoy things that scare us, but we do. I have always enjoyed monsters. I have enjoyed watching monster movies. I have enjoyed reading books about monsters. And I have enjoyed writing about them. You must enjoy them too, or you wouldn't be reading this book.

We are going to look at the most popular of the Supermonsters. We are going to see how the

15

idea of each monster began and how it developed. We are also going to see what people think about these monsters today.

This is to be a journey through the forests of Transylvania and the tombs of Egypt. We are going to visit the laboratory of the mad scientist and the graveyards of the zombies. As I said, none of these creatures exist. But you might want to take a wooden stake and a couple of silver bullets along—just in case.

2

THE VAMPIRE

What is a vampire like? You probably think of him as a tall pale man in a dark suit. He often wears a cape. He looks like he is dressed to go to the opera or to a formal dinner. When he opens his mouth you see two long sharp teeth. They are like the teeth of an animal.

The vampire is not really alive. But then he is not really dead either. He is called the "undead." During the daytime the vampire sleeps in his coffin. At night he gets up and roams the countryside looking for victims. When he finds one he bites it in the neck. Then he drinks its blood. The vampire is compelled to drink the blood of the living. With blood, he can remain in his half-dead, half-alive state forever.

The vampire must return to his coffin before the sun rises. He is afraid of the sign of the cross. The only way to truly kill a vampire is to drive a wooden stake through his heart.

Most vampires are supposed to come from a place called Transylvania. They speak with a slight accent. "I vant to drink your blood." The most common vampire name is Dracula, and he is a nobleman, a count.

That is the picture of a vampire most of us

Bela Lugosi as Count Dracula

have today. It comes mainly from a book called *Dracula*. The book was written in 1897 by an Englishman named Bram Stoker. In 1931 a movie was made from the Bram Stoker book. It starred the actor Bela Lugosi as the evil Count Dracula. The movie was a huge success. Bela Lugosi also played Dracula on the stage and in several other movies.

Since that time dozens of movies about Dracula or Dracula-like characters have been made. There have been television shows about vampires. There is even a vampire-type puppet called the Count on the television program, "Sesame Street." All these vampires look and sound a little like Bela Lugosi playing Count Dracula.

But there were stories of vampires before Bela Lugosi's movie. Bram Stoker did not invent the idea of the vampire either. Vampire stories have been around for a long time. They come from all parts of the world.

In the myths of the ancient Greeks there is Lamia. When Lamia's own children were killed she went mad. To avenge herself she went about killing other children. She also drank their blood and ate their flesh. Once beautiful, she became ugly.

Later, the Greeks developed a legend about a creature called the *striges.* This was a bird-like thing that flew around at night. It also killed children and drank their blood.

The Armenians feared a mountain spirit called Dashnavar. This creature sucked blood from the foot soles of travelers. Dashnavar was particularly dangerous to people while they were asleep. Many travelers slept with their boots on, out of fear of Dashnavar.

Blood-drinking is only one of a vampire's characteristics. Another is that the vampire is a moving corpse. The vampire was once alive, and isn't anymore. But it isn't quite dead because it can get out of its grave. Many thought that anyone who had led an evil life might become a vampire after death. One common belief was that someone who had been a werewolf in life would become a vampire after death.

There are many supposedly true stories about corpses that climbed out of the grave and walked around. Some of the best were written

The vampire in an early German movie

down by an Englishman named William of New-
burgh. William lived over 800 years ago. He was
a churchman and an historian. He swore that all
his stories were absolutely true. Judge for your-
self whether you think this one is true.

The squire of Alnwick Castle was an evil man.
After he died he did not stay in his grave. He
used to wander about in the streets at night. But
this walking corpse continued to rot. The air of
the town became foul from the dead man's body.
As a result, "a terrible plague broke out and
there was hardly a house which did not mourn its
dead." People began to move out of the town

until it was almost deserted. The town council did not know what to do.

Finally, two young men whose father had died in the plague decided to take action. They broke into the cemetery and started to dig up the squire's corpse. As they dug they found the body just beneath the surface of the earth. It was not six feet deep as it should have been. "It was gorged and swollen . . . and its face was florid and chubby, with huge red puffed cheeks, and the shroud in which he had been wrapped was all soiled and torn."

The two young men were angry, not frightened. One struck the corpse with the sharp edge of his spade. "Immediately there gushed forth such a stream of warm red gore that they realized this bloodsucker had fattened on the blood of many poor folk." The body was dragged outside of the town and burned. As soon as this was done the plague ended.

Another man who wrote a lot about real vampires was Augustin Calmet. Calmet was a French monk who lived during the eighteenth century. One of his stories was about a Hungarian soldier named Arnold Paole. Paole said he had been bitten by a vampire in Turkey. People believed that anyone who had been bitten by a vampire would also become a vampire when they died. Paole thought he cured himself by eating earth from the vampire's grave and rubbing himself with its blood.

A short while later Paole was killed when a cartload of hay fell on him. Thirty days after he was buried four persons in the district died mysteriously. The people remembered Paole's story. Perhaps his cure had not worked. Perhaps he had become a vampire after all.

His body was dug up. It had all the marks of a vampire. His hair and nails had grown since he was in the grave. His face was reddish and his veins filled with blood. Blood was splashed all over his winding sheet.

The governor of the district knew all about vampires and how to get rid of them. He ordered that a stake be driven through the heart of Paole's corpse. As this was done the corpse let out an awful shriek. Next, the head was cut off and the body burned.

The same thing was done to the bodies of the

four thought to be the vampire's victims. It was assumed that they had also become vampires. The precautions did not work. Five years later seventeen more people in the village died from vampires.

An official inquiry was held. The authorities decided to dig up the graves of everyone in the area who had recently died. All the corpses that showed signs of becoming vampires were be-headed and burned. Finally, the outbreak ended.

Calmet reported a lot of other vampire stories. Most of them came from countries like Hungary, Rumania, and Poland where belief in vampires was still strong. But Calmet himself did not be-lieve all of the stories. He said that most of the vampire tales were told by people who were poor and uneducated. They had many other supersti-tions as well.

In such places people died from many dif-ferent diseases. There were very few doctors. Often, when a person died, no one knew why. They might blame a vampire for the death.

Calmet also said that people were sometimes buried alive by accident. There was no sure way of telling if a person was dead or alive. A person might merely be unconscious. If such a person were buried quickly, he might revive inside his coffin. Of course, he would quickly die—permanently this time—from a lack of air. But he would struggle before he did. If the coffin was later dug up, it would be obvious that the "corpse" had been moving around. People would be sure they had found a vampire.

Being buried alive is a horrible way to die. We do not know how often it may have happened. But it probably did happen sometimes.

By the time Calmet wrote, most people no longer believed in vampires. But the belief hung on in some villages in Central Europe. It has not entirely died out even today. In 1969 Raymond T. McNally, a professor of history, was traveling in Rumania. He was passing through an area from which many vampire tales had come. He stopped to watch a burial taking place in a village graveyard. The villagers told him they feared the dead girl would become a vampire. So they plunged a stake through her heart. That was less than ten years ago.

Belief in vampires was never very strong in America. But less than 100 years ago there were some vampire cases reported in the state of

Rhode Island. The bodies of people suspected of being vampires were dug up. Then their hearts were removed and burned.

A stake through the heart was supposed to be the most popular method of getting rid of a vampire. The stake was supposed to hold the corpse in the coffin. Another method was to nail the vampire's skull to the coffin with a silver nail.

The vampire had to dig its way out of the grave every night. Some people suggested that a vampire be buried face down. That way it would dig in the wrong direction. The suggestion probably was not a serious one.

When all was said and done, the best way to get rid of a vampire was to burn the body. That is what people who really believed in vampires usually did.

Some vampires were not afraid of a stake through the heart. That was certainly the case with a vampire in the village of Blow in Bohemia. The incident took place around the year 1700.

An evil herdsman had finally died. After he was buried, several townspeople died mysteriously. All the signs pointed to a vampire. People assumed that the herdsman had become a vampire. They dug up his body and drove a stake through his heart. But the corpse only laughed at them. It said it would use the stake as a stick to defend itself against dogs. That night the vampire was on the prowl again.

The people of Blow decided to call in help. They hired a professional executioner. He tossed the corpse into a cart and hauled it outside the town. As the cart bumped along, the body kept shrieking and jerking. Once again the vampire was pierced with a stake. A large quantity of blood gushed out. Then the body was burned and the ashes scattered. The people of Blow were not troubled by the vampire any more.

The vampire is afraid of a cross because a cross is a symbol of good and the vampire is evil. Another good protection against vampires is garlic. People often wore garlic around their necks or hung strings of it in their windows.

The vampire cannot see its reflection in a mirror. A mirror is supposed to be a reflection of the soul. The vampire is the "undead." It has no soul.

Originally vampires had nothing to do with

The vampire in bat shape. This one was in a film called *Brides of Dracula.*

bats. If they changed into anything, it was a wolf. Legends of the vampire and the werewolf were often confused. Then, in the sixteenth century, the Spanish in Mexico discovered small bats that really did drink blood. When stories of these bats reached Europe, people immediately thought of the vampire. The bats were called "vampire bats." After that, the bat became an important part of the vampire legend.

The first great vampire story was written in 1816. In the summer of that year the poet Lord

Byron, another poet named Percy Bysshe Shelley, and Shelley's wife Mary were on vacation in Switzerland. They had rented homes near Lake Geneva. Byron's personal doctor, John Polidori, was also with the group. Sometimes in the evenings they would all get together and tell ghost stories.

Byron began a story about a vampire. But he never finished it. So Polidori took over the idea and developed it into "The Vampyre." The story was very successful, and was also made into a play. Polidori's vampire was called Lord Ruthven.

The next famous vampire of fiction was called Varney. Accounts of Varney's bloody deeds began appearing in England in the 1840s. At that time there was a type of literature called "bloods" or "penny dreadfuls." They were long novels sold in installments. Each week a new installment came out. It cost only a penny or two. The novels were not very well written, but they were filled with bloody and thrilling events. The "bloods" were very popular among the poor. They were the only kind of reading matter they could afford.

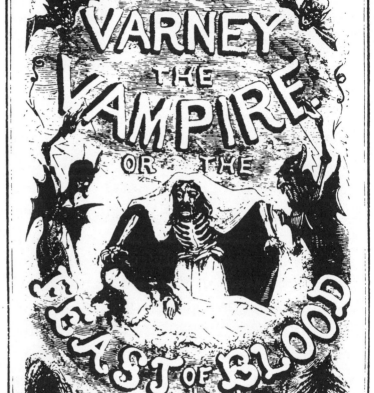

VARNEY THE VAMPIRE; OR, THE FEAST OF BLOOD

A ROMANCE OF EXCITING INTEREST.

BY THE AUTHOR OF
" GRACE RIVERS; OR, THE MERCHANT'S DAUGHTER."

LONDON : E. LLOYD, SALISBURY-SQUARE, AND ALL BOOKSELLERS.

One of the most popular of the "bloods" was *Varney the Vampyre or, The Feast of Blood.* No one really knows who wrote *Varney.* The author was probably a man named James Malcolm Rymer. No one is really sure, since the author's name did not appear on the book. Rymer had

Illustration from *Varney the Vampyre*

Another illustration from _Varney the Vampyre_

written many other "bloods." The story of Varney ran over half a million words. It is the longest vampire novel ever written. In fact, it is one of the longest novels of any kind ever written.

Not all vampires were men. The next great vampire story was called *Carmella.* It is a story about a female vampire. The author was James Sheridan la Fanau, one of the best writers of supernatural fiction who ever lived.

Today few people have heard of Varney or Carmella. But almost everyone has heard of Dracula. Bram Stoker, who wrote the book *Dracula,* said he first got the idea in a nightmare. The story certainly does have a nightmare quality.

Dracula was an immediate success when it was published in 1895. Today, almost a hundred years later, it is as popular as ever.

Dracula, from a Spanish-language vampire film

Stoker used many of the old vampire legends in his story. He said that Count Dracula came from Transylvania. Transylvania is now part of the country of Rumania. It is a place that had many vampire tales.

Stoker had his vampire travel to England in search of fresh blood. Naturally, Dracula had to bring his own coffin along. After Dracula arrives there are many mysterious deaths. At first, people refuse to believe that there is such a thing as a vampire. Then a wise old scientist named Van Helsing recognizes the signs of a vampire. He traces Dracula to his coffin and drives a stake through his heart. The book is really chilling. The Dracula movie with Bela Lugosi is a classic of horror.

Was there ever a real Dracula? That is, was there ever a character in history who was a model for Bram Stoker's vampire? The answer is yes—and no.

When Stoker was trying to pick a name for his vampire he had two requirements. First, the name must sound like it came from Central Europe. That is where most of the vampire legends came from. Second, the name had to sound evil.

There was an historical character who filled both requirements. His name was Vlad Tepov. He was a minor nobleman from Transylvania during the fifteenth century. He had a reputation for being unusually bloodthirsty and cruel. He would have his enemies stuck on the end of sharp wooden stakes. They would just hang there until they died. It was said that Vlad killed 100,000 people.

Vlad Tepov, the original Dracula

The stories of Vlad's savagery are probably exaggerated. Not everyone considers him a villain either. In Rumania he is a hero. Vlad was very successful in fighting the Turks who were invading the land. But to the rest of the world Vlad had a very bad reputation.

Vlad's symbol was the dragon. He was often called *Dracul,* a word that means "dragon." But it also means "devil." The name was then translated to Dracula.

So there *was* a real Dracula. But he was no vampire. No one ever said that he was, until Bram Stoker used his name.

There is another historical character who has a better claim to a vampire's reputation. She was a Hungarian countess named Elizabeth Bathory. She lived during the late sixteenth century.

Countess Bathory was supposed to have had hundreds of people murdered. She used the blood of her victims in magical potions. The potions were supposed to keep her young forever.

The King of Hungary finally heard of what was going on. He put Countess Bathory and her helpers on trial. Many were beheaded. The countess herself was not executed. There was a worse fate in store for her. She was walled up in a small room in her castle. Food could be passed through a tiny hole in the wall. But she was never able to get out. She lived this way for several years, but finally she died.

Later, Elizabeth Bathory was called "the vampire countess." But in her own day she was not known as a vampire. She was just known as a murderess, and a particularly nasty one.

While very few believe in vampires today, vampire stories are more popular than ever. Each year thousands of tourists travel to Rumania to view Vlad Tepov's castle. It is called Dracula's castle, and it has been Rumania's most popular tourist attraction.

3
THE WEREWOLF

People have probably believed in werewolves longer than in any other monster. The werewolf is a man or woman who turns into a wolf at certain times. The word *wer* means "man." Werewolf means "man-wolf."

Practically every nation and tribe has its own stories of people who turn into animals. But these animals are not always wolves. In most of Europe the largest and most dangerous animal a person was likely to meet was a wolf. When someone feared that his neighbor was going to turn into a large and dangerous animal, he thought of the wolf.

The wolf had a very bad reputation. Evil

38

wolves appear in many children's stories. There is the big bad wolf in the story of "The Three Little Pigs." There is another big bad wolf in the story of "Little Red Riding Hood." In fact, the wolf is not mean and vicious, as some people said it was. Wolves stay away from people, unless they are starving or cornered. In both Europe and North America the wolf is nearly extinct today. Efforts are being made to save the few that remain. But the werewolf legends began at a time when people still feared wolves.

In Russia there were plenty of wolves, and people did have stories of werewolves. But there were also bears. So the Russians also had leg-

A werewolf attacks a man

ends about werebears. In Scotland there were very few wolves, but lots of wild cats. There were Scottish legends about people who turned into wild cats.

In India most people have never seen a wolf. But they have seen tigers. So there are legends of wer-tigers. In Africa it is lions, leopards, and hyenas that are most feared. Naturally, there are tales of wer-lions, wer-leopards, and wer-hyenas. China and Japan had werewolves. But tales of wer-foxes were even more common there.

What is behind all of these legends of people turning into animals? Of course we cannot say for sure. It all started too long ago. But we can make some pretty good guesses.

Most primitive tribes have ceremonies in which people dress up as animals. Often they will put on animal skins as part of a dance. The dancers may begin to act like animals. They may even begin to feel like animals. If they are wearing wolf skins they begin to feel as fierce as wolves.

Among the Vikings there was a group of warriors called *berserkers.* The word means "men in bear shirts." The *berserkers* were unusually fierce fighters. They would put on their shirts made of bearskin, and feel wild and brave like bears. In battle they would fight like mad. They would die before retreating.

The word "berserk" is still part of our language. When we say someone has "gone berserk" it means that person is acting wild and crazy. The *berserkers* in their bearskins did not act as if they were human any more.

At one time practically everybody believed in magic. In magic, if something looks like something else, then in a way it becomes like that other thing. To people who believed in magic, when someone put on a wolf skin, then in a sense he became like a wolf.

There was another reason for putting on animal skins. If you wore an animal disguise, no one knew who you were. You could do things without being recognized. Twenty years ago there was a series of brutal murders in Africa. Victims were attacked at night and when they were alone. Their bodies were often badly slashed. It looked as if they had been killed by a wild animal.

Investigators found out that animals were not responsible. The killers were a group of hired murderers called "leopard men." They were paid to kill certain people. Before they went out they put on leopard skins. Their costumes were also armed with sharp steel claws.

These costumes terrified people. Many thought that the killings were being done by leopards. While a "leopard man" was in his costume, no one knew who he was. The "leopard men" also spread the rumor that they really could turn into animals. They hoped to frighten people into keeping quiet about them.

The police finally broke up the gang. Many "leopard men" were imprisoned or executed. But gangs like this in the past could have led to a belief in werewolves or other wer-animals.

In many religions there are tales of animal gods, or of gods who could turn themselves into animals. The ancient Egyptians worshipped a large number of half-human, half-animal gods.

In the religion of the ancient Greeks the god Zeus sometimes appeared as a bull, or even as a swan.

Magicians and witches were said to turn their enemies into animals. There is the fairy tale about the prince who was turned into a frog by a witch. Witches said they could turn themselves into animals when they wanted to. During the witchcraft trials of the Middle Ages, many accused witches said they were able to become cats or other animals.

So, as you can see, the idea of a human being turning into an animal was pretty common.

These are some of the reasons why people believed in werewolves. By the time of the ancient Romans, the werewolf legend had been around a long time. But the first real werewolf story that we have comes from Roman times. It was written down about 2,000 years ago.

It is about a man named Niceros who was on his way to visit a friend one night. A young soldier went with Niceros on his journey. Along the way Niceros suddenly realized that the soldier was no longer by his side. He turned quickly and saw the soldier standing at the side of the

Werewolves in action

road, stark-naked. His clothes were scattered on the ground. The terrified Niceros watched the soldier turn into a huge wolf and run off into the forest.

Niceros, who by now was shaking with fear, arrived at his friend's house. His friend greeted him and told him how a huge wolf had just killed several sheep. Then the friend said that the wolf escaped but was wounded in the neck by a spear before it got away.

As soon as it got light Niceros returned home. As he passed the spot where the soldier had taken off his clothes he saw that the clothes were no longer there. But there was a large pool of blood. At home he found the soldier in bed. A doctor was bandaging a severe wound in his neck. Niceros said he then realized that the man was a werewolf.

The story of Niceros and the werewolf was fiction. It was made up to entertain or frighten people. But it shows that the Romans knew about werewolves. And many of them believed in such creatures as well. The werewolf legend has not changed that much in 2,000 years.

In the Middle Ages people were often accused of being werewolves. Some were tried and executed for the crime of being werewolves. What is more, many of the accused werewolves actually confessed to their crimes. They said that they really did become wolves. While in their wolf state they often killed people.

A very famous case was that of Peter Stubb. Stubb was executed as a werewolf near Cologne, Germany, in 1589. During his trial Stubb confessed to killing and eating at least sixteen people over a period of twenty-five years.

Stubb said that the Devil had given him a magic belt made of wolfskin. When he put the belt on, he was changed into a wolf. Stubb said that he had hidden his magic belt in a valley. But when the judges went to look for it they could not find it. This did not surprise anyone. The judges assumed that the Devil had taken the magic belt away.

Did Peter Stubb really turn into a wolf? Of course not. But he probably thought he did. He must have been a madman who had murderous fits. When one of these fits was upon him he thought he was a wolf and went around killing people. Perhaps he was even a cannibal. When Stubb told people he turned into a wolf they believed him. There are mad murderers in modern times. But no one believes that they turn into wolves—even if they say that they do.

In the days when people believed in werewolves, they did not always believe werewolf confessions. In 1603 a French boy named Jean Grenier claimed he was a werewolf. He also said that he had killed several people. He may have committed murder, but the judges did not believe he had become a wolf.

46

The life and death of Peter Stump, the werewolf

They decided that Jean Grenier was insane. Instead of having him executed, they had him locked up in a monastery. (There were no mental hospitals in those days.)

People loved to hear about cases like that of Peter Stubb. A printed sheet describing Stubb's awful crimes and execution was sold all over Germany. It had many drawings for those who could not read. The sheet was so popular it was translated into many different languages.

47

Putting on a wolfskin belt was not the only way of turning into a wolf. One man confessed that he became a werewolf after eating wolf meat. Another said that he drank water that had collected in the footprint of a large wolf. There was also a magic wolf ointment. It was made of wolf fat and other ingredients. When a person rubbed it on his body he turned into a wolf.

How did werewolves regain human shape? Peter Stubb said he just took off his wolfskin belt. Other werewolves said that they washed in fresh water, or dove into a stream. One said he rolled around in grass or sand. Sometimes being a wolf just wore off after a period of time. In other cases werewolves became human again when they were wounded.

One madman said he was a werewolf, but that his wolfskin was worn on the *inside* of his body. When he wanted to turn into a wolf he just turned himself inside out. The judges didn't believe him. They cut his arm off to see if he had a wolfskin inside. He didn't, but he did bleed to death.

There were supposed to be signs by which a werewolf could be recognized, even when in human form. Anyone whose eyebrows grew together was suspected of being a werewolf. A person whose first finger was longer than his second finger was also suspect. So was anyone who had hair growing on his palms. In fact, anyone who was very ugly or unusual looking, or was badly scratched up, might fall under suspicion.

Sometimes it was a real wolf that inspired the werewolf stories. In the eighteenth century an unusually vicious wolf roamed the Normandy region of France. It was reported to have killed over eighty people. This wolf was so clever at avoiding hunters that people thought it must be more than an ordinary wolf. They thought it was a werewolf.

The American Indians had legends about people who turned into animals. Most European settlers in America did not bring their werewolf legends with them. Only the French who settled in Canada and parts of Louisiana still told werewolf stories. The French called their werewolf the *loup-garou*.

Another werewolf type of creature from France is called the *lupin*. These were strange

A werewolf that was supposed to have killed many people in France 200 years ago

wolf-like creatures that were found around graveyards. They were hard to see, but they could often be heard talking to one another in an unknown language. Unlike the traditional werewolf, the *lupin* was very shy. But sometimes it was bold enough to dig up graves and devour corpses.

People thought there was a connection between werewolves and witches. It was said that the worst of the witches were ''rewarded'' by the

Devil. The Devil allowed them to become werewolves. There was a story from a part of northern Europe called Latvia about a great gathering of werewolves every year. It was believed that thousands of witches came together at Christmastime. Then they were all changed into wolves. They roamed the country, killing men and beasts for twelve days. After that they were changed back into human form for the rest of the year.

Those who really believed in werewolves thought that they looked like real wolves. But today most people think of something else when they hear the word, werewolf. They think of a hairy creature that walks on two legs like a man. It has long teeth and is wild and savage. But it looks more like a gorilla than a wolf. This creature is usually called the Wolf Man. It is entirely a creation of fiction, mainly of the movies.

While there are many werewolf stories, there is no single famous werewolf story. The werewolf was a popular character in English fiction during the last century. The adventures of *Wagner, the Wehr-Wolf* appeared in weekly installments in

An illustration from _Wagner, the Wehr-Wolf_

1846 and 1847. The author of these thrilling tales was G. W. M. Reynolds, a successful writer of "bloods" or "penny dreadfuls." Nearly 125 years ago _Wagner, the Wehr-Wolf_ was almost as popular as _Varney the Vampyre._ But very few bother to read the book today.

A much better book is _The Werewolf of Paris,_

written by Guy Endor. It is a very gruesome story, but it was never as popular as *Dracula* and *Frankenstein.* Most people today have never heard of it.

It was the movies that made the werewolf popular. The first major werewolf movie was called *The Werewolf of London.* It was made in 1935. The film was not based on the book called *The Werewolf of Paris.* In this movie the werewolf is the two-legged hairy creature, rather than a four-legged wolf. The man becomes a werewolf because he is bitten by another werewolf while in Tibet. He changes when the moon is full. In the end the werewolf is killed by a silver bullet.

All of these elements were new to the werewolf legends. It is easier to make up an actor to look like an ape than to make him look like a real wolf. The make-up was very effective anyway. The monster in *The Werewolf of London* is a frightening creature.

The traditional werewolf did not just bite his victims. He ripped them to pieces. There would not be enough left of them to change into a wolf. But the bite of a vampire might turn its victim into a vampire, so the werewolf movies just adopted

53

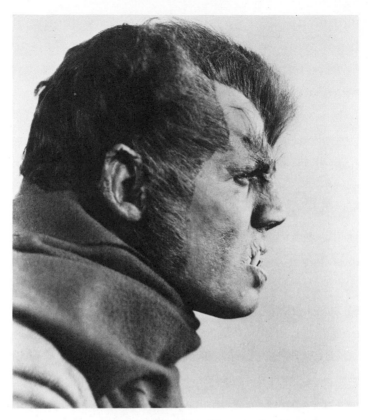

The werewolf from the film _The Werewolf of London_

this and had people turn into werewolves if they were bitten by a werewolf.

The full moon has always had magical associations. There is also an old superstition that some people went crazy when the moon was full. In addition, wolves are supposed to howl at the moon. So it seemed natural to the writers and directors of werewolf movies to have the change from man to werewolf take place at the full moon.

The moon is silvery in color. Silver has sometimes been called the "moon metal." So a creature that changes by the moon can only be killed by the "moon metal"—usually a silver bullet.

The Werewolf of London was a good film. It still is shown on television every once in a while, and it can still scare you. But at the time, it was not very successful. It certainly did not match the success of other monster movies.

The film that made the werewolf a major movie monster was *The Wolf Man.* It was released in 1941. The star was Lon Chaney, Jr., son of a famous star of silent horror films. The real star of the film, however, was the make-up man, Jack Pierce. You can actually watch the transformation from man to Wolf Man up close. First, a little hair was glued on Chaney's face. A few frames of film were shot. Then the camera was stopped. A little more hair was glued on, a few more frames were shot. And so on. It took as much as five hours to film one of these changes. On the

55

Lon Chaney, Jr., as the Wolf Man

screen the scene ran under a minute.

The plot of the film is simple. Chaney plays Lawrence Talbot, a college student and son of a rich landowner. He goes back to the home of his ancestors in Transylvania. (Vampires come from Transylvania, so why not werewolves?)

While walking one night he sees a wolf attack a girl. He drives off the wolf but is bitten before he does. The wolf is not a natural wolf, but a werewolf. At first, Talbot does not know what is happening. Then there are several brutal

56

murders. On the nights of the murders Talbot cannot remember where he was. Finally, he realizes that he is a werewolf. (Why Talbot is changed into the two-legged Wolf Man, rather than a four-legged wolf, is never explained.)

When normal, Talbot is a good man. He does not want to change into the Wolf Man, but there is nothing he can do about it. He can't even kill himself. (In the movies, at least, werewolves are almost immortal.) He asks a gypsy. She tells him that the only way a werewolf can be killed is with a silver bullet or some other silver object. In the end the Wolf Man is killed with a silver-handled cane.

The Wolf Man was a great success, so the movie makers decided that the Wolf Man wasn't really dead after all. He was brought back for a series of other Wolf Man films. But the werewolf as played by Lon Chaney, with make-up created by Jack Pierce, is the werewolf that most of us think of today.

4

THE WALKING DEAD

The vampire is a moving corpse. It is called the "undead." There are two other types of moving corpses that have become popular monsters. They are deader than the vampire because they don't have a will of their own. But they can move. They are the mummy and the zombie. In a sense, both are rather new monsters.

That statement needs some explanation, particularly in the case of the mummy. Mummies have been around for a long, long time. But it is only within the last hundred years or so that they have been regarded as monsters.

A mummy is any dried and preserved corpse.

Preparing mummies in Egypt

Many people have made mummies out of their dead. But those who did it first and best were the people of ancient Egypt. When we think of mummies we almost always think of Egyptian mummies.

59

The mummy was not a monster to the ancient Egyptians. It was a very important part of their religion. The Egyptians expected their soul or spirit to live on after they died. In order to do this they believed that their bodies also had to be preserved.

The Egyptians had a very complicated process for preparing mummies. First, the corpse was cut open. All the internal organs were taken out. These were placed in special jars. Later, the jars were buried in the tomb with the mummy.

The corpse was then rubbed inside and out with various herbs and oils, and dried out. After the corpse was well dried it was stuffed to re-store its original shape. Then more oils were rubbed on the outside of the corpse, and the wrapping began. The mummies of the rich were tightly wrapped in thousands of yards of fine linen bandages. Even the poor managed some wrappings. As the wrapping was going on, still more preserving oils were poured on the ban-dages. The whole process took many weeks.

A lot of people think that the Egyptians had some secret way of preserving the dead. They didn't. All of the fancy wrapping and the rest didn't do much good. Sometimes the oils harmed the body rather than preserving it. The real secret of the Egyptian mummies is that the climate of Egypt is very dry. If dried properly and kept in a dry place, corpses won't rot. The skin will shrink and become hard and leathery. Such a corpse will last thousands of years.

After the mummy was wrapped, it was placed inside several coffins. The richer the dead man, the more coffins he could afford. For the king the coffin might be made out of solid gold. Sometimes these coffins were placed inside a stone burial chamber. The lid to such a chamber could weigh several tons. The chamber was inside a pyramid or tomb cut into the rock. The entrance would be sealed up with tons and tons of heavy stones.

All of this was meant to keep outsiders away from the mummy. It was not meant to hold the mummy inside its tomb. Mummies were not supposed to get up and walk around. How could they? Their feet and legs were wrapped together by yards and yards of bandages. Not only would the mummy have to get out of its elaborate tomb

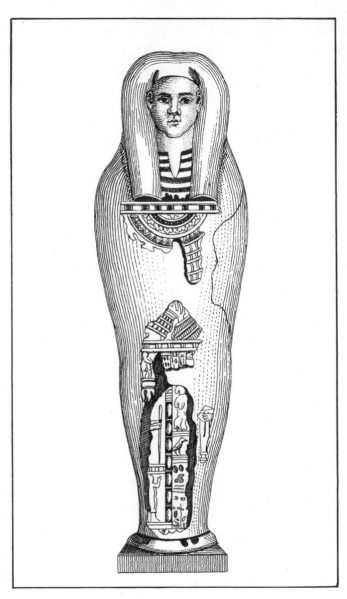

A mummy case

and move away tons of rock, it would first have to unwrap itself. And how could it do that when its arms were bound tightly to its chest?

The tombs of the kings of Egypt were guarded day and night by priests. The priests were supposed to make sure that certain ceremonies for the dead were carried out. There were all sorts of magical spells said at the tomb to keep robbers away. But the mummy itself was not supposed to climb out of its coffin.

None of the precautions worked. Every single royal Egyptian tomb, except one, was robbed. Most of the robberies took place in ancient times. The robbers may have worried about magic. But they never worried enough to stop robbing. The reason for the robberies was quite simple. Egyptian kings were buried with a lot of gold and other precious things.

The robberies got so bad that loyal priests began moving mummies themselves. When they thought a tomb was threatened, they would secretly take the mummy out. They would put it in another, safer tomb. When that tomb was threatened, they would move it again. Finally, the mummies of over twenty of Egypt's most important kings were crammed into one small tomb. That too was found by robbers. But the robbers found it just over a century ago. The Egyptian government heard about the robbers' discovery. They took over the tomb and saved the mummies from being destroyed.

Where did the idea that mummies were dangerous get started? In the first place, 4,000-year-old dead bodies are pretty spooky. If they are well preserved and life-like, it's not hard to imagine that they just might move. The ancient Egyptians also had a reputation for magic.

But what really got people thinking about mummies was the story of "the mummy's curse." That began in 1922. Remember we said that only one royal Egyptian tomb had not been robbed in ancient times? It was the tomb of King Tutankhamen. And it was found in 1922 by two English archaeologists.

Tutankhamen was a very unimportant king. His tomb was small and poor, compared to some of the really great kings. That is probably why the robbers overlooked it.

Tutankhamen's tomb was simple, for an

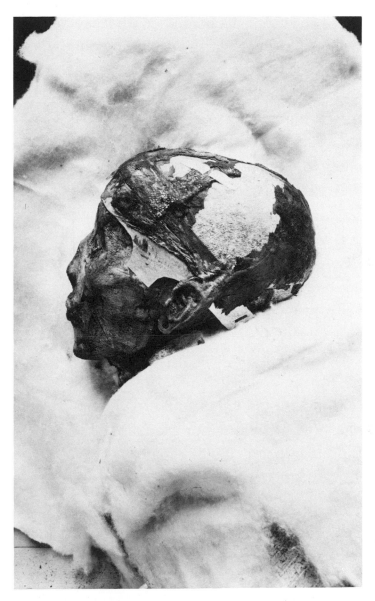

King Tut's mummy

Egyptian king. But it contained what seemed like an unbelievable treasure to the modern world. King Tut, as he came to be called, really was buried in a solid-gold coffin. Some of his other coffins were wood covered with gold. There were all sorts of other golden objects in the tomb. Nothing like King Tut's treasure had been seen before. Naturally, the discovery was a sensation. It made headlines all over the world.

The two men who discovered the tomb were Howard Carter and Lord Carnarvon. Carter was the one who really found the tomb. Carnarvon paid for much of the expedition. A few weeks after the discovery was announced Lord Carnarvon died. It was said he died from an infection caused by a simple mosquito bite. It was also said that all the lights of Cairo went out at the moment Lord Carnarvon died.

A rumor began that the tomb was cursed. The rumor said that there was supposed to have been an inscription carved above the entrance to the tomb. It read, "Death to all who violate this tomb." But there never was such an inscription. The whole idea of "the mummy's curse" was invented by newspapermen.

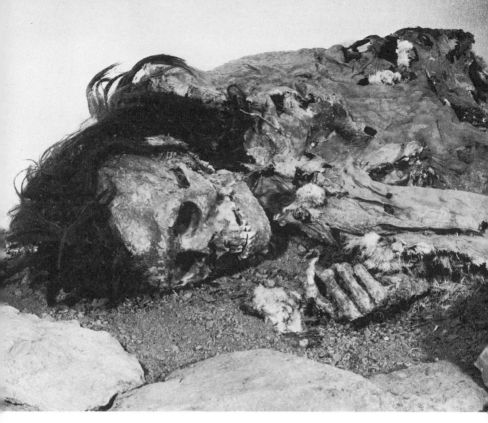

A natural mummy found in the American West

A couple of others who had been involved with the opening of King Tut's tomb died within a few months. That kept the rumor going.

But Howard Carter lived on for another twelve years. He died at the respectable age of sixty-six. There was nothing unusual about his death. And Carter was the one who really found the tomb. In short, "the mummy's curse" is nonsense. But it makes a good story—and plenty of people still believe it.

Still, no one said that King Tut himself was going to get up and walk around. In fact, his mummy was in terrible shape. Even before the discovery there had been stories about walking mummies. But they never caught on. The discovery of King Tut's tomb did make people more interested in ancient Egypt. The story about "the mummy's curse" frightened them a bit.

The idea of a walking mummy was really created in a movie called *The Mummy.* It was produced in 1932, and starred Boris Karloff. Once again the make-up artist was Jack Pierce, who created the make-up for the Wolf Man and the Frankenstein monster.

In the original mummy picture, Karloff looked like a very wrinkled man. That is after he was unwrapped. He could move about and talk quite normally. He was extremely smart and extremely evil. But he was a walking mummy, and at the end of the film he crumbles into dust.

The movie was a success, and the mummy was brought back in other films. In sequels the

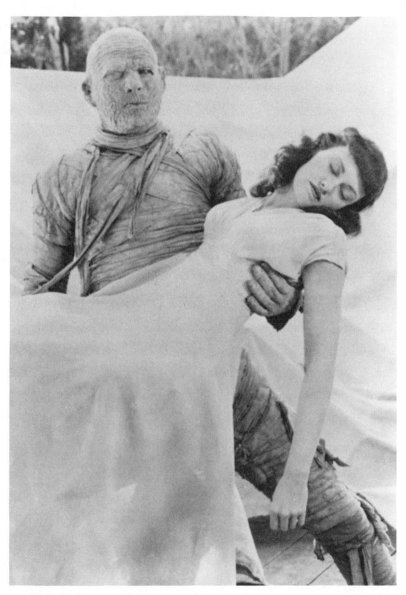

A Hollywood mummy

The mummy in a British movie

mummy became more robot-like. In *The Mummy's Curse* Lon Chaney, Jr., played the mummy. He is never completely unwrapped. He stumbles along dragging yards and yards of linen bandages behind him. The mummy in these later movies doesn't have much of a mind left. He is usually under the control of an evil priest.

The Aztecs of Mexico also had mummies. They are not as famous as the mummies of Egypt. But when a Mexican film producer wants to make a mummy movie he uses an Aztec mummy for the monster.

In the later movies the mummy behaves very much like a zombie. The zombie is another monster that has often appeared in the movies. But the zombie is not a monster created for the movies alone. The mummy movies are based on the idea that the Egyptians had magical ways of making dead bodies move. They didn't—and never claimed that they did. But on the island of Haiti there is a belief that some people do have the power to make corpses move. This moving corpse is called a "zombie."

The zombie is a corpse brought back to a form of life by a *houngan*. The *houngan* is a voodoo priest. Voodoo is a popular religion on Haiti. It is made up of many different elements. Magic is one of them. The priests of voodoo are sup-

A symbol for the voodoo god of death

posed to have magical secrets. Among their secrets is a method of making dead bodies move again.

No one can agree on what the word "zombie" means. Nor does anyone seem to know exactly when people started believing in zombies, or why. Most zombie stories are fairly new.

The zombie is much like a robot. The *houngan* is supposed to create zombies in order to do work for him. The zombie has no mind or will of its own. It is entirely under the control of the *houngan*. Zombies are very strong and can work without ever getting tired. They are perfect slaves. Zombies will also kill on the *houngan's* command.

According to some legends, zombies can be brought out of their death-like state if they are given salt. When they realize what has been done to them, they may turn against the *houngan*. The *houngans* are very careful about showing their zombies to strangers.

There were stories that crews of zombies were hired out to work in the fields at night. Some people thought that bakers employed zombies. Bakers usually made their bread at night. The fires of the ovens glowing in the darkness made an eerie sight. Some people suspected that evil things must be going on. They thought that one of the reasons bakers worked at night was so that people would not see who was helping them.

Probably the most famous zombie story was

first told in 1935. A young girl had died and been buried. Three years later one of her friends saw her at work in a shop. While the girl moved stiffly and looked blank and vacant, the friend was sure of her identity.

An investigation was launched. It was found that the girl's body was missing from its grave. It had been stolen by a *houngan* who had turned her into a zombie. The zombie was rescued and sent off to France. The story continues that her brother visited her there years later. She was being kept in a convent. This is supposed to be a true story.

Another woman who was supposed to be a zombie was actually kept in a hospital in Haiti. She was seen there by many people. Photographs of her were even published.

This woman had appeared one day on a farm. She could barely speak, and acted very strangely. Some people recognized her as a relative of the owner of the farm. She was supposed to have died years earlier. She was taken off to the hospital. Later, the dead woman's husband was accused of poisoning her and then paying a *houngan* to turn her into a zombie.

The truth of the story is probably less sensational. This zombie was almost certainly a woman who was mentally defective. She must have wandered away from wherever she had been kept. She also must have looked at least a little like the dead woman. When she turned up on the farm, people were frightened. They identified her as a zombie. Since she could not speak or think very well, she could not correct them. Perhaps some people had resented the dead woman's husband. They were ready to blame him for her death.

Zombie stories usually concern the poor and uneducated. They are the most devoted to voodoo. But sometimes the rich and educated also tell of meeting zombies. There is the tale of a rich man whose car broke down in front of the house of a *houngan*. The *houngan* told him that the breakdown was no ordinary accident. He invited the man inside. Then he showed him a zombie. The man recognized a good friend who had been dead for about six months. The man offered the zombie a drink. But the *houngan* stopped him and warned him of the terrible dangers of being kind to a zombie.

One of the most sensational zombie stories appeared in a book called *The Magic Island.* It was written by an American named W.B. Seabrook. A *houngan* named Joseph owned several zombies. Joseph's wife was looking after the zombies. One day, without realizing what she was doing, she gave them some salted biscuits to eat. The salt made them wake up from their deathly trances. They realized that they had been walking corpses. They made straight for the graveyard, brushing aside all who tried to stop them. They threw themselves on their graves and tried to dig themselves back into the earth. But they rotted before they could complete the task.

Seabrook related the story as if it were true. He had a lot of other zombie tales in his book. But there is no proof to back up any of them. Seabrook was just repeating a lot of tall tales that he had heard.

Even today there are some *houngans* who claim that they have zombies. An English investigator named Francis Huxley wanted to see one. But none of the *houngans* he met would agree to show him a real zombie. Huxley finally decided that they didn't have any.

Sometimes zombies are faked, in order to fool people. One man reported going to a graveyard one night to watch a *houngan* make a zombie. He saw the *houngan's* assistant dig up a coffin. The *houngan* said some magic words over the corpse in the coffin. He poured some unknown liquid on it, and the corpse got up out of the coffin. It looked very real.

The next day the man went back to the grave-yard. He took another look at the grave the

A collection of zombies from the film *White Zombie*

A scene from *I Walked with a Zombie*

houngan's assistant had dug up. There was an air hose leading from the surface down to where the coffin had been. The man inside the coffin had been alive all the time. The air hose gave him air to breathe. The whole ceremony had been a show.

Some people think that *houngans* have drugs that can make people act as if they were zombies. But no one is sure of this.

Do people in Haiti really believe in zombies today? That is hard to say. Some families are supposed to guard the graves of their relatives for the first few weeks after burial. After that, the corpse would be too rotted to be of much use as a zombie.

Most Haitians probably don't believe in zombies. But they will tell zombie stories anyway. Haitians love telling supernatural stories, in order to amaze and frighten their audiences. Perhaps they frighten themselves sometimes.

There have never been any famous zombies in written fiction. But the zombie has been used in a number of movies. Probably the two best are *White Zombie*, which came out in 1932, and *I Walked with a Zombie*, which came out in 1943. These two films were set in Haiti. There are a whole host of other zombie films. They have been set everywhere from Cambodia to outer space.

5

MAN-MADE MONSTERS

In the chapter on the vampire we described what happened in the summer of 1816. That is when a small group of poets and their friends were vacationing in Geneva, Switzerland. To pass the time they decided to write ghost stories. That meant stories on any supernatural subject. This gathering produced the first major vampire story in the English language, the one called "The Vampyre." But a far more important creation was begun that summer. It was the novel, *Frankenstein* by Mary Wollstonecraft Shelley.

The idea for *Frankenstein* may have started

during an idle and rainy summer. But the book was meant to be more than just a scary story. It is about a young German scientist named Baron Victor von Frankenstein. Frankenstein wants to find out how life begins. In fact, he becomes obsessed with the idea. He is not trying to create a monster. On the contrary, he hopes and believes that his discoveries will benefit mankind.

Because his ideas are so unusual he is expelled from his university. He returns to the village of Ingolstadt, ancestral home of the Frankenstein family. Here, in a specially constructed laboratory next to the family castle, Frankenstein continues his experiments. In order to get the parts of human bodies needed for his experiments, Frankenstein and his assistant must rob graves.

Finally, he succeeds. He is able to produce a living creature from the pieces of dead people. Frankenstein hoped that his creation would be a perfect specimen of humanity. But from the moment it comes to life he realizes something is very wrong. The creature is hideously ugly. Frankenstein also fears that it may be evil. Later events prove this fear to be correct.

Most people make a mistake about the book. They think that the monster creature's name is Frankenstein. But Frankenstein is the name of the scientist. People may also call the creature "the monster," which it certainly was. But the creature has a name, though hardly anyone remembers it. The name is Adam.

Adam is the name of the first man created by God in the Bible. Victor von Frankenstein was creating life. He was, in a sense, playing God. He was certainly attempting to do something that most people thought only God could do.

Today we just call the book *Frankenstein.* But Mary Shelley had a longer title for it. She called her book *Frankenstein or A Modern Prometheus.* Prometheus was a figure in ancient Greek mythology. He stole fire from the gods and gave it to mankind. For this crime of defying the gods, Prometheus was hideously punished. In the book Victor von Frankenstein is also hideously punished.

Frankenstein's monster creature escapes from the laboratory. Later it kills his brother. But Frankenstein's monster is not just a mad or mindless killer. It is highly intelligent, and can talk. The creature explains to Frankenstein that it kills because mankind has rejected it. It says it did not ask to be brought into the world. It is angry at Frankenstein for having created it at all. There is a great deal of justice in the monster's claim. In fact, it is the monster who is really the tragic hero of the book.

Much of the book concerns Victor von Frankenstein's attempts to escape the revenge of his monster creation. Ultimately the monster kills its creator. Then it disappears among the icebergs of the Arctic.

The book was quite successful when it was first published. It has remained popular ever since. It is the only one of Mary Wollstonecraft Shelley's books that is still remembered today. It has also been made into a movie. In fact, it has been made into movies many times.

The first Frankenstein movie was made way back in 1910. It was produced by Edison Studios. The studios were owned by Thomas Alva Edison, the man who invented the light bulb and many other things, including a practical motion picture camera. Edison's *Frankenstein* was one

Boris Karloff as the Frankenstein monster

of the earliest films made. It was not a great success. Another production by another studio was tried in 1915. It was entitled *Life Without a Soul.* Once again, it was a failure.

The Frankenstein that everybody remembers was produced in 1931 at Universal Studios in Hollywood. Universal produced all the great monster films in those days.

To play the part of the monster Universal picked an unknown British actor named William Henry Pratt. Pratt was using the name Boris Karloff. Originally Karloff didn't think much of the part. The monster had no lines to speak. All it did was grunt and mumble and walk around like a robot. The make-up was so heavy that no one would ever recognize Karloff. And it was un-comfortable. He had to wear a suit that weighed 48 pounds. Still, jobs were scarce and Karloff needed the money. So he took the part. He was lucky he did. The film was an immediate suc-cess. It made Boris Karloff the number one star of horror films for a generation.

Mary Shelley described the monster as being abnormally tall and thin. It had pale skin and a generally corpse-like appearance. When we think of the Frankenstein monster we think of a greenish-skinned creature with a flat head, stitches all over its face, and a couple of electrodes sticking out of its neck. That monster was the creation of Universal's great make-up artist, Jack Pierce. Underneath all that make-up was Boris Karloff, who really wasn't very scary looking at all.

The scriptwriters didn't stick to the plot of the book either. In the book the monster is created by chemical means. In the movie Frankenstein uses electricity. One of the best scenes in the film comes near the beginning. Frankenstein brings his creation to life during a raging storm. He uses the electricity from the lightning to power his machines.

There are many other changes from the book. For some reason Frankenstein's first name was changed from Victor to Henry. Yet even in the film we can sympathize with the monster. It is not an evil creature at first. But the monster in the film cannot explain itself, because it cannot talk. It just makes noises.

The Frankenstein monster is supposed to be burned up in a fire at the end of the film. But the

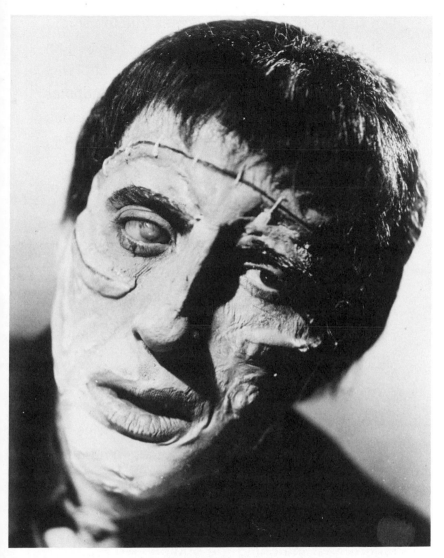

Christopher Lee in the British version of Frankenstein. Lee is made up to look more like the monster in the original book than Karloff was.

film was such a financial success that the studio just had to bring the monster back. The sequel was called *The Bride of Frankenstein* and was released in 1935. In this movie the monster wants companionship, so Frankenstein decides to make him a female monster. The title of the film is really misleading. It should be called *The Bride of the Monster.* Frankenstein himself already had a bride.

By the way, in the original Mary Shelley book, Frankenstein does try to make a mate for his monster. Usually sequels are not as good as original films, but *The Bride of Frankenstein* is an exception. In some ways it is even better than the original Frankenstein movie.

The Frankenstein monster was brought back again and again in other films. The part was played by different actors. Often the movies had several monsters like the Frankenstein monster, Dracula, and the Wolf Man, in one film. There have also been several television versions of Frankenstein. None of the sequels come anywhere near matching the original two Frankenstein films.

The vampire and the werewolf started as legends. People believed in them, and later they were put into books and movies. The Frankenstein monster is entirely a creation of fiction. But Mary Shelley was influenced by some ancient beliefs, and ancient fears, when she wrote her book.

The idea of artificial monsters goes back at least as far as the ancient Greeks. The Greeks had a legend about Talus, a man made out of brass. Talus had been constructed by Hephaestus, a god of fire and craftmanship. The job of the brass man was to protect the island of Crete. This he did very well.

Talus was kept alive by a vital fluid which ran through a single vein in his body. A powerful sorceress named Medea was able to cut the vein. The vital fluid flowed out and Talus died.

Another man-made monster of legend was the *golem.* The golem is a figure in Jewish legend. It is a creature made of clay or stone. It is made to move by magic. There are many versions of the legend of the golem. One is set in Prague in the sixteenth century.

The golem was supposed to have been created by a famous rabbi. It was to be a protector of the Jews, who were being severely persecuted. But the golem was impossible to control and had to be destroyed.

The golem has been used in many horror films and will probably be used in many more. But it has never really become a popular movie monster. Everybody knows what the Frankenstein monster is supposed to be. Very few would know what the golem was supposed to be.

During the Middle Ages there was a practice called "alchemy." The alchemist's main goal was to turn base metals into gold. But another thing that some alchemists were supposed to try to do was to create artificial life. The artificial man was usually called a *homunculus.* Generally this creature was very tiny, and could be kept in a bottle.

Several alchemists were reported to have actually created a homunculus. Formulas for making an artificial man have been published. Needless to say, none of them worked. But the alchemists' reputation as wonder-workers lingered on.

90

The golem in a 1920 German film

Alchemists were often in trouble with religious authorities. It was felt that they were dealing with things that were forbidden. By trying to turn base metals into gold or to create artificial life, the alchemist was trying to play God. Alchemists denied they were playing God. But people believed that they were anyway.

Alchemists also had a reputation for being evil. No one was sure what they were doing in their secret laboratories. The alchemists themselves insisted that they were merely seeking after nature's hidden truths. Many were persecuted, and some executed, despite their denials. And despite the fact that they never succeeded.

Certainly Mary Shelley had alchemists in mind when she created the character of Victor von Frankenstein. Like the alchemists of old, he dared to try and expand the limits of human knowledge.

In the movie, *The Bride of Frankenstein,* there is an evil character called Dr. Praetorius. He has created miniature living figures that he keeps in bottles. This is clearly based on the old homunculus of alchemy.

Was there a single character who served as a model for the monster-making scientist Victor von Frankenstein? Some people think that Mary Shelley was inspired by a legend about an old German castle outside of the city of Frankfort. The castle is said to contain the tomb of a medieval knight. This knight, according to the legend, fought a man-made monster that resembled a wild boar—and lost.

Mary Shelley had traveled widely in Europe. She may have heard the legend. Or there may have been some other German castle which prompted her to set the beginning of her novel in Germany.

There was one gruesome activity of the nineteenth century that undoubtedly did influence the author of *Frankenstein.* That was body snatching. Doctors found that it was almost impossible to teach anatomy because there were not enough corpses available for dissection. Some countries actually outlawed dissecting human corpses for any purpose. As a result, many doctors resorted to robbing graves—or at least buying corpses from those who did.

There is a body snatching scene in many horror stories

Body snatching became a fairly profitable business. The body snatchers were also called "resurrectionists" or "sack-em-up men." They would sneak into a graveyard shortly after a funeral. They had to get bodies quickly, before they began to rot. They would dig up the grave, take out the body, then fill the grave in again. If they did their work well, no one would ever know the body had been stolen.

In fact, the body snatchers performed a useful service. Doctors could never have been adequately trained without the corpses the body snatchers delivered. But most people regarded the practice with absolute horror anyway. A body snatching scene was used in many books. It has also become a standard part of many horror movies.

Body snatching was also a symbol of how far the scientist would go to increase his knowledge. He was ready to violate the graves of the dead. By doing this he pushed aside common decency and human feelings. He would stop at nothing to reach his goal. Victor von Frankenstein himself was forced to steal bodies to make his monster.

6

HUMAN MONSTERS

The chief villain in many fairy stories of long ago was the evil witch or sorcerer. The witch or sorcerer knew magic. Through magic the villain could call up demons or cast a spell.

Then people stopped believing in magic. A new villain replaced the witch or sorcerer in stories. This villain was the mad scientist.

Dr. Victor von Frankenstein was one of the early examples of the mad scientist. Originally, Frankenstein wasn't mad, and he wasn't evil. But his knowledge made him powerful and what he did had evil results. By refusing to give up his experiments, no matter what happened, he was, perhaps, a little bit mad.

After the publication of *Frankenstein*, the mad scientist became the chief creator of monsters. Next to Victor von Frankenstein, the best known mad scientist in written fiction is Dr. Henry Jekyll. Dr. Jekyll didn't make an artificial monster. He made himself into a monster that he called Edward Hyde.

Dr. Jekyll and Mr. Hyde were the creation of Robert Louis Stevenson. Stevenson wrote the book about them in 1885. Stevenson said he got the idea in a dream. He locked himself away in his study and wrote the book very quickly.

The original Stevenson story has both a moral purpose and a surprise ending. The purpose was to point out that there was good and evil in everyone. The surprise was that the good Dr. Jekyll and the evil Mr. Hyde were one and the same person. Both the purpose and the surprise have been forgotten today. *The Strange Case of Dr. Jekyll and Mr. Hyde* is thought of as a horror story, and a good one.

Dr. Jekyll is trying to explore the good and evil sides of man's nature. He develops a formula that splits the two sides of his personality. He then discovers that the evil side—the Mr. Hyde side of his personality—is much stronger than he imagined. Hyde begins to take over. He commits terrible crimes. Finally, Hyde fears he will be hung for his crimes, so he kills himself. In the story the truth is discovered among Dr. Jekyll's papers. It is revealed to the reader only in the last few pages.

Stevenson described Hyde as being pale and dwarfish. People around him got the impression that he was deformed, but nobody quite knew how. When Mr. Hyde got into the movies he was transformed into a real monster. Everyone knew what was wrong with him. In some film versions Mr. Hyde looks a lot like the Wolf Man.

There may be more movie versions of Dr. Jekyll and Mr. Hyde than of any other monster story. The first important Jekyll and Hyde film was made in 1920. The great actor, John Barrymore, played the title roles. As Dr. Jekyll drinks his formula, he begins to make faces. Then he falls to the floor. He rises up wearing his ugly make-up. The handsome Dr. Jekyll has been transformed into the horrifying Mr. Hyde.

The next major Jekyll and Hyde film starred

Fredric March. It was made in 1932. In this version the transformation takes place right before your eyes. There is no cop-out, with the actor falling on the floor out of camera range. March won an Academy Award for his performance.

Spencer Tracy played Jekyll and Hyde in a 1941 version of the movie. Tracy didn't use a great deal of make-up. Even as Hyde, he looked quite human, but quite evil.

Hollywood then tried *Son of Dr. Jekyll* and even *Daughter of Dr. Jekyll.* There were a couple

Fredric March as Mr. Hyde

of other attempts at sequels. None was very successful. The story was even turned into a television musical, but not a very good one. Recently, the tormented Dr. Jekyll and the evil Mr. Hyde have been left in peace.

A mad scientist of a different type is the hypnotist. For over two centuries hypnotism has had a bad reputation. Some people thought a hypnotist could completely control his subject. Today we know that hypnotism is nowhere near as powerful as people once thought it was.

Dr. Caligari and his robot-like subject, Cesare

But a mad hypnotist and his subject were featured in one of the earliest and best horror films ever made. The film was called *The Cabinet of Dr. Caligari.* It was made in Germany in 1920. When it was released it was a sensation. It has influenced horror films down to the present day.

This influence is particularly obvious in one scene. The evil Dr. Caligari sends his robot-like subject, Cesare, to kidnap the heroine. Cesare sneaks into her bedroom and carries her off in his arms. Naturally, she is wearing a long white robe.

H.G. Wells was an early writer of science fiction. One of his most successful tales was *The Invisible Man.* It was about a scientist who discovers a formula that makes him invisible. Unfortunately, the formula also drives him mad.

The story was first made into a movie in 1933. It gave movie makers a chance to use some spectacular special effects. The invisible man first appears completely bandaged up like a mummy. But as the bandages are unraveled they reveal that there is nothing inside—at least nothing that can be seen. There were several sequels to the invisible man, and other films and TV shows on the invisibility theme.

Monster fans have a great deal to thank H.G. Wells for. Not only did he give us the invisible man, he also gave us several other monster firsts. The perfect mad scientist appeared in his story, *The Island of Dr. Moreau.* It was about a scientist who was creating monsters in his secret island laboratory. That was also made into a movie and inspired many imitations.

The Wells story, *War of the Worlds*, was about the invasion of monsters from Mars. A very realistic radio drama was made from the story in 1938. It was so realistic that some people thought an invasion was actually taking place. They grabbed their guns and were ready to defend their homes against the monsters from Mars. The story also inspired a huge number of other stories and movies about invading monsters.

Getting back to human monsters, there is nothing obviously supernatural about the famous "phantom of the opera." He is a person who is horribly disfigured. This has driven him mad. He lives in the miles of tunnels beneath the Paris Opera House. He spends his time helping those he likes and killing those he does not like. At times, though, the phantom does seem to possess powers far beyond the normal.

The Phantom of the Opera was written in 1911 by the French author, Gaston Leroux. It would be very hard to find an English translation of the book today. The book would probably be forgotten completely if it had not been made into a marvelous movie—in fact, two of them.

The first was a silent version made in 1925. It starred Lon Chaney as the phantom. Chaney was a master of make-up. His make-up for the phantom was the best he ever created. Throughout much of the film he wears a mask. In one scene the heroine, who has been captured by the phantom, rips off his mask. The phantom's hideous skull-like face is revealed. That always brings gasps from the audience.

The Phantom of the Opera was remade in 1944. This time the phantom was humanized. He was supposed to have been a violinist whose face had been burned by acid. When the mask is ripped off, it reveals a grotesquely scarred face.

Left: Lon Chaney as *The Phantom of the Opera,* with mask . . .

. . . and without mask

Below: The phantom from a later film version of *The Phantom of the Opera*

The scene is still terrifying. There have been other attempts to remake this classic, but none have been very effective.

The Phantom of the Opera gave rise to a whole army of deformed and disfigured madmen of the movies. There is always a scene in which the disguise is torn away and the terrible true face of the monster is revealed. The scene always works.

7

MONSTER ANIMALS

The people of the ancient world told stories of a great number of monstrous animals. Most of the stories were just that—stories. No one was supposed to really believe them.

One of these monsters from the myths of the ancient Greeks is the *chimera.* This creature was supposed to have the head and front parts of a lion, the body of a goat, and the hindquarters of a dragon. Sometimes it is shown as a three-headed monster, each part having its own separate head.

To make matters worse, the chimera had a fiery breath. It was able to burn up anything that came near it. The monster was finally killed by the hero, Bellerophon. The hero was riding the winged horse, Pegasus. This allowed him to stay clear of the chimera's fiery breath.

The word "chimera" is still a part of our language. It means any wild or unfounded illusion. To say that someone is chasing a chimera means that the person is chasing an impossible dream. That seems to have been the way that the Greeks felt about this monster as well.

But not all of the monster animals of Greek mythology are entirely imaginary. Some were based on facts, though the facts were exaggerated for the purpose of storytelling. One such monster is the *centaur.* This is a creature that was half-man, half-horse. Greek mythology is full of centaur tales. Sometimes the centaurs are good, sometimes evil.

There is no real centaur, and there never was. But the myth is based on something. That something is the mounted nomads that from time to time swept down on Greek-controlled lands. In very early times the Greeks did not ride horses. They only used donkeys or horses to pull carts. The first time the Greeks actually saw people riding horses, they must have been astonished.

The nomads rode very well. It looked as though horse and rider were two parts of the same creature. That is how the legend of the centaur must have begun.

The same sort of legend sprang up in South America centuries later. When the Spanish invaded South America, they brought horses with them. The South American Indians had never seen a horse. The sight of a man riding a horse terrified them. They thought that horse and rider were a single centaur-like creature. When they saw a man fall off his horse they thought the monster had broken in two.

An even more frightening monster from Greek mythology is the *minotaur*. This was a half-man, half-bull creature owned by King Minos of the island of Crete. It was so terrible and wild that Minos kept it hidden in a maze beneath his palace. It ate only human flesh.

Each year, according to the legend, seven young men and seven young women were thrown into the maze. They were never seen again. Eventually the monster was killed by the hero, Theseus.

Though the legend sounds utterly fantastic there may be a grain of truth in it. In ancient times Crete was the center of an important and powerful civilization. We call the people who lived in Crete at that time Minoans.

In studying the remains of Minoan civilization, archaeologists have found many paintings and statues of bulls. Obviously, the bull was an important symbol to the Minoans. There are also pictures of people jumping over bulls. Perhaps the Minoans once had a ceremony where people really were sacrificed to wild bulls. Memories of such sacrifices could have survived in the terrible legend of the minotaur.

When scientists began digging up the royal palace in Crete they got a shock. There was no order or plan to the building. It seemed to be a jumble of rooms. It would have been very easy to get lost in such a building. Perhaps that is where the idea of the maze which held the minotaur began.

The Greeks were not the only people to have tales of monster animals. From the Middle East come the legends of Sinbad the Sailor. These are full of fantastic beasts. Probably the best

110

known is an enormous bird called the *roc.* The roc was supposed to be so large that it could carry elephants in its talons.

The legend of the roc has many origins. It probably began with exaggerated accounts of eagles. These birds are large and fierce. They have often inspired legends.

Later, Arabian sailors may have brought back giant eggs from their voyages. The eggs were nearly the size of a basketball. They were not the eggs of a roc. They were the eggs of the elephant bird, an enormous ostrich-like bird. The elephant bird is now extinct. But a few hundred years ago elephant birds were plentiful on the island of Madagascar. Sailors often carried away elephant bird eggs as souvenirs. That is one of the reasons the elephant bird is now extinct.

People also reported that they had seen a feather from the roc. What they saw was not a feather at all. It was a leaf from a palm tree that grows on Madagascar. The leaf looks a bit like a giant feather.

It is not hard to imagine that sailors told tall tales of seeing the giant bird. Then they backed up their stories with the giant egg and the giant feather. A lot of people would have believed them.

The American Indians told stories of something they called the thunder beast. This was a huge animal like a buffalo except bigger. No one had ever actually seen this monster. But a lot of people had seen its gigantic bones. The Indians thought the thunder beast had something to do with the rain. The bones were commonly found after rainstorms.

In a way these Indian legends were quite correct. The bones did belong to giant animals. But these animals were extinct. They had died out thousands of years before. The bones were buried deep in the earth. Sometimes a strong rain or a flood would wash away the soil and expose the bones on the surface.

The Indians also had tales of a gigantic bird. It was called the thunderbird. These legends may have begun with the eagle, but more likely they were inspired by the California condor. This bird is a giant vulture. It is one of the largest flying birds alive today. It is still very impressive, though it is nowhere near as large as the legendary thunderbird. The California condor is very rare today. Its habitat must be carefully protected to save it from extinction.

The legends of some monster animals are fairly recent. In different parts of England there are legends about the black dog. These stories are only a couple of hundred years old. That is recent as far as legends go.

The black dog is a huge and supernatural hound. It appears on lonely roads and is bad luck to anyone who sees it. Some legends even say it can attack solitary travelers. Sir Arthur Conan Doyle used the legend in one of his most famous Sherlock Holmes stories. The story is called *The Hound of the Baskervilles.*

Most of the monster animals that we think of today are even more recent. They are entirely fictional. They were created in the imaginations of movie makers and science fiction writers.

The best, and most popular, monster animal from the movies is King Kong. The film *King Kong* was first released in 1933. It was an immediate success. It ranks as one of the three or four best monster movies of all times.

113

The man who first originated the idea of King Kong was Merian C. Cooper. Cooper had been in Africa photographing gorillas. He got the idea that a film about a giant gorilla loose in New York City might be a money maker. First he thought he could use pictures of real gorillas. Later he found this would not work, so he switched to model gorillas.

Many different-sized models of King Kong were used in the filming. The model was set up and one frame was shot. Then the model was moved slightly and another frame was shot.

King Kong

Each step Kong made required twelve separate exposures. It took an entire day to photograph thirty seconds of film. In addition to Kong himself, the movie also had model dinosaurs and other strange creatures. The process was slow, and expensive. But it was worth it.

The final scene of *King Kong* is one of the most celebrated in movie history. The giant gorilla, carrying blonde actress Fay Wray in one hand, climbs to the top of the Empire State Building. There he is gunned down by airplanes—but not before he manages to swat some of the planes out of the sky.

Because of *King Kong's* success there were many, many sequels and imitations. The film was even remade in a new version in 1976, over forty years after the original movie appeared. In the 1976 version King Kong climbs to the top of the World Trade Center in the final scene. The Empire State Building was the tallest building in New York in 1933. Today it is the World Trade Center.

The idea of the gorilla as a monster did not originate with King Kong. It goes back a long way. When Europeans first began hearing tales

115

of gorillas, they did not know what to think. They could not decide whether the creature was ape or man. They thought it might be some sort of wild man. Many of the stories told of how fierce the creature was.

When Europeans first encountered living gorillas they were terrified. The huge apes roared and beat their chests. The gorilla got the reputation of being the most ferocious beast in the

A dinosaur from the film *The Lost World*

jungle. This reputation was still around when the movie *King Kong* was made.

Today we know that all the stories about ferocious gorillas are just nonsense. The gorilla is very strong. It can be dangerous if it is frightened or annoyed. But ordinarily the gorilla is a very gentle and lazy creature. It likes nothing better than to sit in the shade, eat, and sleep eighteen hours a day.

Will this new view of gorillas affect the popularity of King Kong as a monster? Only time will tell.

Ever since dinosaurs were discovered, people have thought of them as monsters. They certainly were monstrous in size. They were probably monstrously dangerous too. But the dinosaurs all died out long before there were any people on the earth.

Writers of fiction have often used dinosaurs in their stories. Sir Arthur Conan Doyle wrote a story about finding living dinosaurs. It was called *The Lost World. The Lost World* was first made into a movie in 1925. Dinosaur models were used.

Godzilla meets King Kong in a Japanese film

That was not the first time model dinosaurs appeared on the screen. In 1917 the Edison company produced a short film called *The Dinosaur and the Missing Link.* It used the same type of models used much later in *King Kong.* The 1925 version of *The Lost World*, however, was the first time that dinosaurs became popular movie monsters.

There were plenty of dinosaurs in *King Kong*

118

too. But they were overshadowed by the giant gorilla. Other movies that had dinosaurs somehow or other invading the modern world had only modest success. There was no really great movie dinosaur until the Japanese presented *Godzilla, King of the Monsters* in 1955.

Godzilla looks sort of like a fat tyrannosaurus. But he isn't just big and strong. He also has "atomic breath." He can destroy a whole building just by breathing on it.

In the first film Godzilla was a real monster in every sense of the word. He was in the process of destroying Tokyo when he himself was destroyed. But he was so popular that the film makers brought him back again and again. In one of the other Godzilla films there was even a giant ape called—you guessed it—King Kong. Godzilla became sort of a friendly monster. The films often ended with a fight between Godzilla and an unfriendly monster.

Monsters are very popular in Japan. Japan makes a large number of movies about monster animals like Godzilla. Monsters of one sort or another are also very popular on Japanese television.

The monster in *The Creature from the Black Lagoon*

One other notable film monster appeared in 1954. It was *The Creature from the Black Lagoon.* The creature is supposed to be some sort of prehistoric man-fish. No models were needed for this monster. The creature was played by a man wearing a scale rubber suit and a fish-like mask.

The creature comes up out of a mysterious South American lagoon. Naturally, it carries off the heroine in one scene. Finally, it is wounded and lumbers back into the water. But the creature recovered and made two more films.

There were a great number of monster movies which featured ordinary creatures that had

A giant ant from the film *Them*

We will never run out of monsters

grown to monstrous size. There were films about giant ants, and giant crabs, and giant moths, and giant praying mantises. Even the giant shark in the movie *Jaws* really falls into this group.

In the movies a lot of monsters come from space. Some of them, like the Thing, are intelligent vegetables. Others, like the Blob, have no shape at all.

As long as monster movies are popular, new monsters will have to be invented. In films people seem to want bigger and better (or worse) monsters. At times the movie makers have had to strain to keep up with the demand for more horrors. But the human imagination is equal to the job. We will never run out of monsters.

INDEX

125